Dear Parent:
Your child's love of reading starts here!

Every child learns to read in a different way and at his or her own speed. Some go back and forth between reading levels and read favorite books again and again. Others read through each level in order. You can help your young reader improve and become more confident by encouraging his or her own interests and abilities. From books your child reads with you to the first books he or she reads alone, there are I Can Read Books for every stage of reading:

SHARED READING
Basic language, word repetition, and whimsical illustrations, ideal for sharing with your emergent reader

BEGINNING READING
Short sentences, familiar words, and simple concepts for children eager to read on their own

READING WITH HELP
Engaging stories, longer sentences, and language play for developing readers

READING ALONE
Complex plots, challenging vocabulary, and high-interest topics for the independent reader

ADVANCED READING
Short paragraphs, chapters, and exciting themes for the perfect bridge to chapter books

I Can Read Books have introduced children to the joy of reading since 1957. Featuring award-winning authors and illustrators and a fabulous cast of beloved characters, I Can Read Books set the standard for beginning readers.

A lifetime of discovery begins with the magical words "I Can Read!"

Visit www.icanread.com for information on enriching your child's reading experience.

Pinkalicious®
Tutu-rrific

For Lilly
—V.K.

The author gratefully acknowledges the artistic and
editorial contributions of Daniel Griffo and Natalie Engel.

I Can Read Book® is a trademark of HarperCollins Publishers.

Pinkalicious: Tutu-rrific
Copyright © 2014 by Victoria Kann

PINKALICIOUS and all related logos and characters are trademarks of Victoria Kann. Used with permission.

Based on the HarperCollins book *Pinkalicious* written by
Victoria Kann and Elizabeth Kann, illustrated by Victoria Kann

Library of Congress catalog card number: 2014935753

ISBN 978-0-06-218796-3 (trade bdg.) — ISBN 978-0-06-218795-6 (pbk.)

14 15 16 17 18   PC/WOR   10 9 8 7 6 5 4 3 2
❖
First Edition

I Can Read!

BEGINNING
1
READING

Pinkalicious®

Tutu-rrific

by Victoria Kann

HARPER
An Imprint of HarperCollinsPublishers

Alison and I giggled as we tried

to balance on our toes.

Tomorrow we were going

to ballet class together!

I was pink with glee.

I had never taken

a ballet class before,

but Alison had.

"You'll love it," she said.

"We twirl and jump through the air

and spin on our tippy-toes."

"What fun!" I said.

"What's your outfit like?" I asked.

"It's a purple tutu,"

said Alison.

"What does yours look like?"

I laughed and said, "Guess!"

The next day, I got ready:

I wore my pink tutu,

pink slippers,

and pink bows in my hair.

Mommy took me to class.

When we got there, I thought I saw

a purple tutu.

"There's Alison!" I said.

I ran inside to catch Alison.

There were people all over!

I thought I saw a flash of purple

run into a room.

"Alison, wait!" I called.

But Alison didn't hear me.

I followed her into the class.

I couldn't spot her

with all the dancers.

Just then, the teacher walked in.

"Okay, everyone!" she said.

"Take your place at the barre."

I'd have to find Alison later.

"Time to warm up," said the teacher.

"First position," she called.

I looked around the room.

Everyone was moving their feet.

Heels together, toes apart.

This was easy!

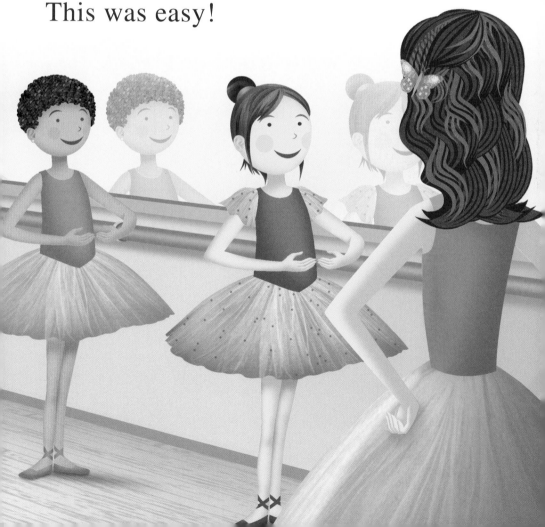

"Plié," the teacher sang.

The ballerinas bent their knees,

so I did, too.

Piece of cake!

"Very good," said the teacher.

"Now, let's go over

the dance we learned last week."

I didn't know the moves,

but I wasn't worried.

Ballet seemed really, really simple.

The teacher put on some music.

The dancers moved their arms,

first up, then down.

Then they kicked their legs

up and down.

I followed along just fine.

Suddenly, the music got faster.

The girls skipped in a circle

and jumped in the air.

I was stuck in the middle,

not sure what to do.

Everyone moved so quickly.

I couldn't keep up!

When I hopped, they kicked.

When I kicked, they swayed.

"Hold on!" I cried.

But no one could hear me!

I looked around for Alison,

but she wasn't there.

It was a girl who looked like Alison.

I had made a mistake.

I knew I had to say something.

I stopped dancing and raised my hand.

"Excuse me," I said.

"I think I'm in the wrong class!"

Just as I put my hand up,

the dancers jumped up high.

"Beautiful!" said the teacher.

She didn't see me!

I tried to get out of the circle,

but the dancers linked arms.

I tried crawling through their legs,

but the dancers hopped up and down.

"Wait!" I shouted,

but nothing helped.

I was trapped between tutus

with no way out.

"Get ready for the grand finale!"
the teacher called out.

I gulped.

The girls spread out their arms
and started twirling.

"Oh!" I said, happily surprised.

They were spinning!

I could do this!

I took a deep breath

and twirled and whirled

and spun around.

I was spinning so freely,
I didn't notice that everyone
had stopped.

The teacher looked at me, confused.

"You!" she said.

"You're not in this class!"

"Uh-oh," I whispered.

I was sure I was in trouble.

Instead, the teacher just smiled.

"You must be in the wrong room,"

she said.

"I'll have someone walk you to

the beginner class.

But first, could you spin again?"

I twirled around once more.

"You're so graceful!" said the teacher.

"Keep practicing and soon

you will be in my advanced class."

In the beginner class,

I told Alison what happened.

"What was it like?" she asked.

"It was tutu-rrific!" I said,

and did a pirouette.